To: Adam

From: Mom 2013

NOTES TO MY SON

BEFORE YOU GO

Vesna M. Bailey

OMNI Publishing
Leamington, Ontario, Canada

Dedication

For my children Stephen, Lauren and Karyn
Who inspire me every day,

My parents
Who have guided me and loved me every day,

My husband
Who has been an amazing father to our children every day.

No bird soars too high
if he soars with his own wings.
William Blake

Introduction

Every mother and son has their own story to tell – yet at certain milestones, their story has a juncture common to all.

I initially wrote this book for my own son as he prepared to leave home for university where he would pursue his love of flying and aviation. Like many mothers I had a checklist in hand to help me gather things he would need for residence life, but I found there were so many more pressing and urgent things I needed to remember to pull from the shelves in my heart – a mother's last minute words that are meant to last a lifetime.

The mission of this book is to capture all that we as parents aspire to impart to our sons in preparing them for their "solo flight" – words that will inspire them, guide them, and anchor their footsteps on solid ground as they spread their wings to soar as high as their dreams will carry them.

Although we well know our heartstrings will always keep our child near, we also know that the path they will travel from now on will very much be their own journey – and we must allow them to feel it and walk it freely, while still being there to celebrate their footsteps along the way.

For a son to leave behind his childhood is certainly a remarkable milestone. After much soul searching we realize the only truly meaningful and adequate things measuring up to this occasion that we could authentically pass on to him are the bits and pieces of ourselves, borne of our own life tapestry. With these comes our boundless wish that he will be blessed with a happy and full life – one filled with good health, joy, laughter, kindness, compassion, justice, and peace, that he experience the best of humanity and life's goodness – and that he may lead a life worthy of all these things.

Life is not all a fairy tale. It truly isn't. But we must know and trust that our sons will have many amazing chapters that will carry them through the valleys and thunderstorms, only to emerge atop a glorious mountaintop. We now take a back seat knowing they will continue to amaze us with their potential to grow and learn, to love and to feel.

We say these words to our sons with almost incomprehensible joy, yet how bittersweet they feel:

"Thank you for letting me travel with you this far. I am so proud of you – you have no idea! ...Now, fly away, soar high, and knock their socks off!"

A Class Act

To be what we are, and
to become what we are
capable of becoming is the
only end of life.
Robert Louis Stevenson

Love yourself.
Believe in yourself.
 You are amazing!
Bright, caring, loving, fair, genuine, funny, insightful,
level headed, focused, unique, and ... handsome!

Sculpt a concept of spirituality that you are comfortable
 with and abide accordingly through living a good, honest, joyful,
and kind life.

 Be yourself.

 Be proud.

Carpe diem.
(Seize the day.)
Horace (65-8 BC) Roman poet

Care.
Be kind, sensitive, compassionate and generous.

Be genuine.

Get excited! Dream it! Live it!

Live like you mean it - with passion and fortitude.

SUNFLOWERS
always TURN TO THE SUN

As they say, in truth life is like a box of chocolates - you never know what you are going to get. React carefully, choose wisely, handle setbacks gracefully, and stay excited about the limitless possibilities - forge ahead confidently.

There is nothing mystical about achieving a full and happy life - find your purpose; live a kind, honest and good life; be productive, creative, self-sufficient; be open to love and being loved.

To find your purpose in life is not always easy - be patient as you allow it to change and evolve. Time will transform it to its intended form. Trust.

Our aspirations are our possibilities.
Samuel Johnson

What will be your legacy?
Live a life that will mirror your potential.

Dare to stand alone.

Life is the simplest of math equations;
what you put in is what you get out -
in every aspect of your life.

Honor your principles, always.

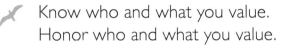

Know who and what you value.
Honor who and what you value.

Live your life with integrity and never risk losing self-respect.

Set your standards high -
if you don't gauge them high for yourself,
no one else will.

Know where you came from.
At the crossroads, that knowledge will help point you
in the direction you need to go.

Be your own best friend.
Let mistakes and regrets lead not only
to a lesson learned but also self-forgiveness.

Gentle is the wind that brings songs of praise
but ferocious is the storm that comes to question us.
Trust that all things considered you did your best,
and peace is yours to keep.

How will the success of your life be measured?
Only your answer counts.

Respect your fellow man - their views, challenges,
perspectives, upbringing, weaknesses
and vulnerabilities, strengths and virtues.

Every problem contains the
seeds of it's own solution.
Anonymous

Tolerate the different, the difficult,
and the unpleasant in the world as much as you can.
Be patient.

Look deeply into people's eyes -
every fiber of their being is there like
a chapter for all the world to read.
Tune in!

Try not to become bitter with the world -
know that for every cruel atrocity
we hear of on the morning news,
somewhere, somehow, someone's life is
bearing witness to life's goodness.

Your time may be limited,
but your imagination is not.
Anonymous

Life is full of little miracles -
take time to notice them, to find them.

Pay homage to them.
You are a miracle!

Allow yourself the time and space to admire
and savor the gifts around you -
a sunset, a deed, a piece of art,
a friend's trait, someone's talent,
an animal's instinct.

All things considered, time unfolds as it ultimately must.
Safeguard your conviction that life is good.

Know that time itself is the only true

commodity in life - invest all that you can!
Don't waste it.

Try not to waste time on negative thoughts and energy -
be generous to understand, forgive, accept, and move on.
What have you learned?

When you wake up in the morning, expect it will be a great day -
amazingly it works most of the time!

Stay aware of things in your life to be thankful for.

Smile a lot - help light up the world!
Only good things can come of it.

Each day try to give at least one other person
a reason to smile, from ear to ear.

 Revel in the simple pleasures of life;
not everything has to be exotic and expensive.

Live freely but responsibly.

Balance is the key to everything.

Show someone you believe in them - every day if you can.

Keep track of yourself - once each year jot down the
highlights of your year; things you have accomplished,
learned, done, and the new dreams that have been awakened
within you, and because of you.

Wherever you go, whether it be across the globe
or across the street, notice how the love in a mother's arms
knows no skin color, the walls of a home know of the same joys
and sorrows no matter where they stand, and the symbols of worship
echo the same promises. We all belong. We all fit.
The sunflower turns to the same sun
no matter where it grows.

IT'S EVERYBODY'S BUSINESS

- At Christmas time visit one lonely person.

- Remember the underprivileged.

- Sponsor a child in a Third World country.

- Donate to charity.

- Donate a food basket to someone in need.

- True compassion knows no social class, no race, no ethnicity. Be a living witness to this conviction whenever you are entrusted with the opportunity.

Listen with your heart,
Feel with your eyes,
Do with your soul.
Mom

Be aware of what is going on in the world.
 Try to fit it into the big picture of what you already know.
Make it a goal to learn more when you have time.

Catch the daily news highlights.
Try to flip through at least the Saturday edition of a good newspaper;
be aware of the world around you.

Help an elderly person cut their grass, offer a ride,
help them plant a garden.

Remind yourself often that the aged were once young and vibrant too,
bursting with dreams, vision and hope, bravery and sacrifices, laughter
and mischief. Their earned wisdom that they offer to you
is a treasure and a privilege.

There is no greater gift you can offer to an
elderly, lonely person than to lend them
a bit of your time and your ear.
To feel old, spent, and easily discarded is a cruel place.

Savor the opportunity to spend time
and learn from an interesting person.

The worst sin towards our
fellow creatures is not to hate them,
but to be indifferent to them;
that's the essence of inhumanity.
George Bernard Shaw

In conversations, listen and participate.
 Honour the other person by showing interest
or familiarity with the subject matter.

 Contribute to your community in some way.

Vote.
 Make yourself heard.
Know what you stand for.

Don't litter or pollute.
 Recycle.
Respect the earth and everything that lives therein.

FUN STUFF!

 Treat yourself now and then - you deserve it!

 Act on your inspirations when they occur.
With time, the moment fades and the magic is forever lost.

Create.
It doesn't matter what.
 Your hands are the vessels by which
hidden treasures and talents will emerge.

Walk with a spring in your step, a twinkle in your eye,
 a smile within your heart, a vision within your grasp.
Let it show!

Dream!
Build sand castles in the sky!

Give "tight" hugs.

Give firm hand shakes.

Stand up straight.

Treat yourself to nice cologne.

Cheer loudly.
Clap passionately.

Drink good wine.

 Tip well.

 Learn how to waltz.

 Don't be short on flowers in your life.
Give them freely and often.

MORNING BELL!

To live is a privilege,
To be aware is wise,
To learn is a duty.
Mom

Life is an adventure in learning -
discover it, live it, savor it, love it.

Strive for knowledge - it truly is powerful and invigorating.
It is the breath of life.

Never lose your sense of wonder.
Nurture it, each and every day.

Once in a while gaze up at the clouds -
surely you will discover fairies and dragons,
pyramids and oceans; it's all up to you to see it.
The canvas is always there - you just have to pick up the paintbrush.

Remember, not everything worth learning has to be immediately useful and applicable. All knowledge has some hidden worth.
It's all good!

Read!

Even ten minutes a day.

Keep books all around you.

Turn the television off once in a while and flip through a book.

Over time, create your own home library.
Undoubtedly it will become one of your most loved possessions.

Include books by foreign authors.

Own the best dictionary you can afford.

Force yourself to learn at least a bit about the classics -
literature, art music, philosophy, mythology, history.
Give yourself a basic education in the liberal arts.

Branch out - read a good variety of things.
Allow yourself to develop familiarity with a broad range of topics -
life for you will then be that much more interesting and invigorating. You
will find many more people and places interesting.
And you will be that much more interesting.

Read autobiographies/biographies of the people
that have left their mark on the world.
Sports, social movements, history, entertainment,
religion, science, the humanities, your personal heroes, etc.

Through books you can travel the universe and get to know the most
intricate threads of the tapestry of mankind while uncovering more
pieces of your own being. It is all connected -
we are all connected.

Try to learn one new word every day.
It is actually hard not to!

Just trust yourself,
then you will know
how to live.
Johann Wolfgang von Goethe

Force yourself if you have to, but visit an art gallery/museum
and go to a symphony or a theater at least once a year.
 Listen to classical music at least once in a while -
even if it is only ten minutes a month.
In time, you will come to appreciate it more and more.

Get even more familiar with the physical world -
look at an atlas once in a while and try to find five new countries,
islands, mountains, rivers. Imagine the worlds at your fingertips.

Travel the world as much as you can.

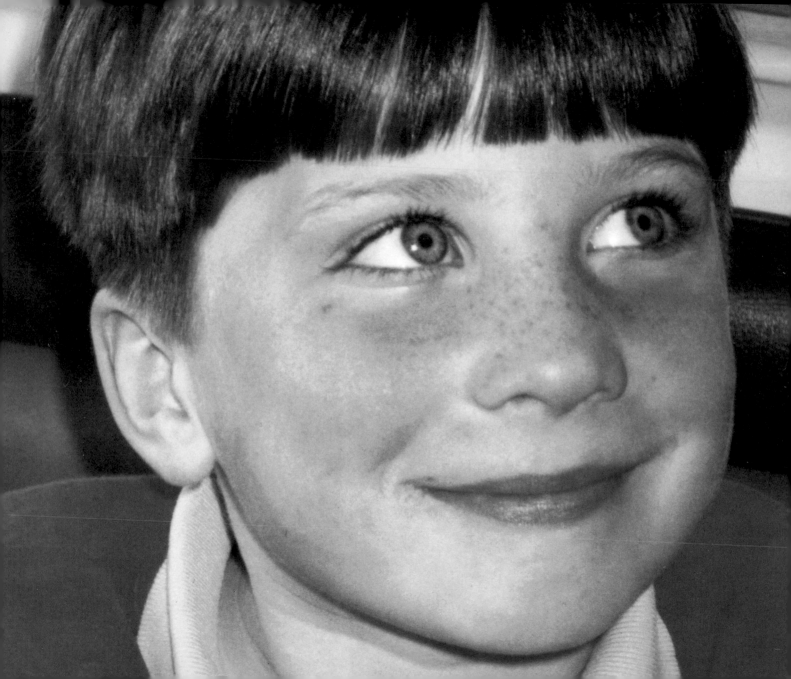

Keep a list of things you would like to learn more about one day, when you have time.

 Learn a new language - or just try!

Life is wonderful! It truly is full of wonders
but the most amazing wonders of the world
are those that lie within your own world.
There is no greater fortune than
being lucky enough to recognize them on time.

MORE
A B Cs!

Put an effort into everything you do; it shows if you do and if you don't.
Put a deserving effort into living.

Have a life plan. Keep a focus on your goals.
Recognize distractions and your vulnerabilities.

Strive for self-discipline.

Do not procrastinate - get it done!
You will sleep better and you will not have to fall into
panic mode or chaos management.

Go confidently in the
direction of your dreams.
Live the life you've imagined.
Henry David Thoreau

Do not get behind.
Sometimes it is impossible to catch up.

Go to bed on time.

When you are overly tired or hungry - eat and sleep.
Don't be miserable and take it out on others.

Force yourself to work early in the day.
You will be more productive and you will accomplish more.

Delegate when it makes sense.
Don't carry the world on your shoulders.

Be organized.
Use labels, files, filing cabinets.
The initial time and energy you invest will be well worth the effort
when you have to find something in a hurry.

Excuses have many uses but none that will serve you well.
Honor your integrity.

Celebrate and acknowledge the small steps as you climb them.
Keep the end in sight - and the beginning.

Live within your means.

 Budget.
Allot for gifts, entertainment, travel, living expenses, and rainy days.

 Invest wisely.
If it sounds too good, fast and easy, it probably is.

An ounce of spontaneity is the spice of life.
Strive for a balance between being purpose driven
and 'falling for the moment.'

A TOUGH DAY

Some choices are more difficult
to make than seems imaginable ---
Search for the compass pointing
you to the greater good and set sail,
Keeping faith as your rudder,
Hope as your wind,
Belief as your anchor,
Peace and acceptance as your harbor.
Mom

W. Zawadski

Count your blessings regularly.

 Life is not always easy, but it is good.
Don't let go of that.

 Accept that some losses are necessary.

When you are feeling most vulnerable
remember your family that loves you,
your friends that cherish you,
your achievements that speak of you,
your uniqueness that defines you,
and the universe that embraces you.
Then go be of service to someone else.
Your doubts will be put to sleep.

When things seem overwhelming be thankful that you are alive,
healthy and competent enough to be given
the opportunity of this challenge -
and know it is only temporary.

Know that self-doubt is only a glorious invitation
to accept the challenge. Conquering it transforms you
and lifts you, to once seemingly impossible heights.

Know it is OK to be scared sometimes.
It only means you have a healthy respect for,
and a healthy perspective of the situation at hand.

There is nothing heroic or intelligent
about being afraid to ask for help.
We are all smart and strong but there are times when we all need help.

Remember, sand castles fall down
only to give you an opportunity to practice building new ones.
Realize that they're not half-fallen down,
but even with only one grain of sand remaining,
they're left half-standing and already half-built.

Know that whenever a door closes,
it will lead to a new door opening in due time.
This is only an opportunity for you to prepare for your grand entrance.
Be patient.

Don't begrudge the painful or difficult times in your life;
this is when you were doing some of your best growing
and you were becoming the person that you are.
Challenges give us strength, validate our character,
attest to our capacity to learn,
and affirm the love and support around us.

Do not feel sorry for yourself for too long.
Look around - there are so many who would
readily trade spots with you.

Do not be quick to blame others. Look within first.
You will be surprised how often it is ourselves

who are to be held accountable.
This is just another generous opportunity for us to learn and grow.

If you strongly dislike your job, course of study, etc. -
change it! Even if it requires more education, training,
or a cut in pay. If you don't you will be miserable
and you will make those around you miserable.

Always keep the power to make choices.
Think long term when you consider all your options.

Laugh and cry without shame.
To feel is to be alive and bears witness to humanity.

I KNOW
YOU KNOW,
but...

All things are difficult before
they are easy.
Thomas Fuller

Stand up straight.

Exercise!
Stay fit, look fit, walk fit.

Eat only when you are hungry.

Eat responsibly.
It's up to you to take care of your body -
it has to last you a long time.

Put a napkin on your lap during meals.
Use a knife.
Hold your fork properly.
Twirl spaghetti in a spoon.
Don't lick your fingers - use a napkin.

Write your own thank you notes, promptly.

Shower every day; look clean, smell clean.

Clothes and manners
do not make the man;
but when he is made,
they greatly improve
his appearance.
Henry Ward Beecher

 Try to keep your room tidy.

Wash your sheets regularly.

 Don't walk around wrinkled - iron, or buy wrinkle free.
Take your clothes out of the dryer
when they're still warm and hang or fold them.

 Re-vamp your closet once in a while;
give any clothes to charity that haven't been worn in a year.

Keep up with your laundry.
Sort the darks (cold water),
whites (hot water),
and brights (warm water).

Own at least one good suit.
Own a good pair of brown and
a good pair of black shoes -
keep them clean and polished.
They tell a story about you.

Don't wear socks with sandals.

Don't wear white sports socks with nice pants.

CAN WE TALK?!

Do not be quick to judge others.
Everyone has his or her own story to tell.

Look for the good in people.
Don't expect perfection.
Choose to forgive trespasses.
It is not always easy to do that but it is often necessary.
Ultimately it is the only road that leads to finding peace within you.

Honor those around you by showing them respect
through your choice of words and actions.
Know your boundaries.

Remember, self-respect and respect from others

is something that has to be earned.
One might say we are always at work in this regard.

Love is unconditional but respect is earned.

It is a lot easier never to lose the respect of others
than it is to earn it back.

Give and take in all your personal and business relationships.
It's about winning at life - not about winning

the competition or argument.
Be aware of your motives.

Be willing to compromise, as long as it does not involve
sacrificing your values and integrity.

Work hard at listening.
Ninety percent of a relationship is determined by how well you hear.

Choose well who to discuss politics and religion with.
Don't be tempted to convince.
Be prepared to accept that others are entitled to,
and maybe even justified in,
having a differing opinion from your own.
Even in disagreement you must still maintain respect.

Consider your friendships sacred.
Nurture them and cherish them.
Acknowledge and recognize the blessing of each person in your life.

Cradle and protect the confidences entrusted to you -
as long as in doing so, no harm will come to anyone.

Remember, people can forgive,
but it's truly hard to forget.

Be clear in communicating your thoughts and needs.
No one can read your mind.

Beware of gossip.
Even if a word of it were true it serves no good purpose
to push a person who already may be stumbling.

Validate others through paying attention to them.
When you truly pay attention to another person
you are in effect validating every fiber of their being.
How amazing that a gift so invaluable is truly so simple to offer.

Let others know - say it or write it - just how much you care
about them or appreciate them: whether they are a mechanic who
fixed your car or a friend who got you tickets to a concert.
Don't assume they already know.

Give people feedback.
Let them know they matter.
Deserved compliments go a long way.

Remember important dates.

Don't forget you are your sister's and brother's hero.
Be a fan club for them: support them, validate them, praise them,
encourage them, honor their individuality.
Remember their birthdays.

The Girl in
Your Life

Be a gentleman - always.

Don't use foul language around ladies.

Open the door for ladies.

 Stand up and offer your seat to someone older than you, a female of any age, a mother with child.

Like in the 'old days', stand up and pull out a lady's chair when she is getting up from the table.

Choose a girlfriend who lets you be you, loves your company
but can also stand apart from you, one you can laugh with
and have a ton of fun with.
A sense of humor is more important than you would ever guess.

Choose a girlfriend you find interesting and intellectually stimulating.

Treat your girlfriend, one day your wife,
like a princess - because she is a princess.

If you are contemplating marrying a certain girl be sure
you accept her and love her 'just the way she is.'
You cannot change anything about her, nor should you want to.

Keep the expectations of your relationships real -
one person cannot fulfill everything in you.
That's why we are blessed with friendships.

It has been said that guys fall in love with their eyes
but girls fall in love with their ears.
They need to hear you say it - at least every so often.

The dating game rules:
You pay! Yes, girls can vote but they like
having their dinner paid for too!

Get dressed up once in a while for a 'night on the town'!

"Just because!" is the best reason to give someone a kiss on
the forehead, a tight bear hug, or a flower. (That includes your mom!).

Things and people are
beautiful if you love them.
Jean Anouilh

THE CLOSING ACT

With all it's sham, drudgery, and broken dreams, it is still a beautiful world.
Be cheerful. Strive to be happy.
Max Ehrmann

Always know your family loves you and supports you - no matter what.

Know that our home will always be a place
where you can return to and hang your heart.

Honor your father and mother.

Cherish your sisters and your brothers.

I HAVE A DREAM

MARTIN LUTHER KING, JR.

THE MARCH ON WASHINGTON

FOR JOBS AND FREEDOM

AUGUST 28, 1963

- Make a difference.

- Be the difference.

- Live a noble existence.

- Celebrate YOU!

It matters.
You matter.
Live a life that matters.
Mom

Although it was not perfect, I hope my life
was a good enough classroom where you have
heard this all before.

I love you. Adam!

Call home. *often!*

About the Author

Vesna Bailey was born in Dubrovnik, Croatia and came to Canada as a child. She now lives in Leamington, Ontario, with her husband and their three children. Her passion for writing is inspired by her children, and being a mom is an unparalleled joy in her life. Prior to embarking upon writing, Vesna enjoyed a rewarding career as a Speech-Language Pathologist. Her first book, *Notes To My Son Before You Go*, won a 2008 IPPY Book Award, and was awarded First Place in the 16th Annual Writer's Digest International Self-Published Writing Competition, Inspirational Category. One year later, *Notes To My Daughter Before You Go* won the same IPPY Medal. For Vesna, the opportunity to donate a portion of the proceeds from book sales to charitable causes adds an added dimension and meaning to her journey in writing.

Another of Vesna's passions is amateur photography and some of the photos in her books are from her own collection. Her books also contain purchased professional photography, as well as a small number of her favorite photos from albums of close family friends. She is forever grateful for their generosity.

Writing a fiction novel is in Vesna's future plans.

Awards for
NOTES TO MY SON BEFORE YOU GO

Independent Publisher Book Awards 2008
Bronze Medal Winner – Gift/Holiday/Specialty category

16th Annual *Writer's Digest* International Self-Published Book Awards
1st Place Winner – Inspirational category

Also by Vesna M. Bailey

NOTES TO MY DAUGHTER BEFORE YOU GO

Independent Publisher Book Awards 2009
Bronze Medal Winner – Inspirational category

NOTES TO MY SON BEFORE YOU GO

www.NotesBeforeYouGo.com

copyright © Vesna M. Bailey, 2007

First Published by Walkerville Pubishing Inc. Windsor ON Canada
First Printing – Spring, 2007
Second Printing – Fall, 2007

Published by **OMNI Publishing**
30 Lathrop Lane   Leamington ON Canada N8H 1E4
e-mail: vesna.bailey@notesbeforeyougo.com

Third Printing – Spring, 2010
Fourth Printing – Summer, 2012
all rights reserved

ISBN: 978-0-9784408-0-0

Cover and Book Design by Walkerville Publishing Inc.

Printed in China